RACIST OR NOT

 What is Racism to you?

What is the definition of Racism to you?

No, I will not put the definition of Racism here because; Racism is a broad topic, and a confusing topic. Thus, Racism take away your right and rights as well as, freedom from you in my view because; _NO ONE CAN TAKE RACE OUT OF RACISM._ People will forever hate.

Say something derogatory about some, and you are labelled a Racist.

If you don't like a specific race, you're a Racist.
If you don't like Gays, you're a Racist.

Say Jews are pathological liars, you are labelled a racist, banned, spreading hate, and more. Yet, no one sees the lies written about God in the Bible and the lies; willful and categorical lies told on God.

Therefore, Racism is like unto the Covid-19 vaccines of Death. You have no rights and freedom because; the Governments of the Globe, Corporate Greed, Pharmaceutical Greed, and more take your rights and freedom from you.

You are forced to accept their lies, their deceit because; _ALL THAT IS WRONG WITH THEM AND ABOUT THEM, IS BEING FORCED UPON YOU; WE THE CITIZENS OF THE GLOBE._ Thus, the different viruses, and diseases manufactured in labs to kill, and do kill.

NO ONE SHOULD BE FORCED TO LIKE YOU PERIOD.

Everyone now a days is racist but for me; _PEOPLE HIDE BEHIND RACISM, AND I REFUSE TO HIDE BEHIND A LABEL._ Like I've said in other books; _IT'S MY GOD GIVEN RIGHT TO NOT LIKE YOU AS LONG AS I DO NOT HARM YOU._

You cannot force people to like you because not everyone is likeable. Therefore, I will not hide behind any label for anyone.

The fact is _PEOPLE ARE RACIST PERIOD._ I too can be, and I am in some of these books thus, I tell you when I am being racist. However, I will not promote hate or stand for anyone using these books to promote hate. I refuse this. _I also refuse to tell anyone to hate another human being. It is not right, it is wrong._

When I tell someone to hate you based on whatever, I am sinning. I am taking your rights and freedom from you, and I refuse to take your rights and freedom from you. I also refuse to add more Sin to my already Sin Record.

Jo Mersa Marley feat. Black Am I – <u>NO WAY OUT</u>

Protégé feat. Lila Ike & Agent Sasco – <u>NOT ANOTHER WORD</u>

I know hell and the demons of hell.
I know what happens in the grave to some.

I know the beating I will get in the grave so hell no. I truly love my life.

Why should I give anyone including the Demons of Hell the victory over me?

<u>*Different people have different cultures and it's okay if they don't like you.*</u> The problem in all of this are/is humans.

<u>"YOU CANNOT FORCE PEOPLE TO LIKE YOU."</u>

In my view. You are the problem because, <u>*YOU SEEK ACCEPTANCE FROM THOSE WHO DISLIKE AND HATE YOU.*</u> You are wrong when you seek acceptance from those who dislike and hate you.

Stay your ground and stay true to you.

Why fight to be included in racist societies, communities, countries, families, and more?

And please truly do not use God thus, you want to be accepted by Demons; those who hate you.

I do not have to accept or like you if you are Gay, a Muslim, a Christian, Roman Catholic, Arab, Babylonian, White, Black, Chinese, so-called Jew, a Transgender It Thing, and more.

I refuse to fight for wrongs. *THEREFORE, IT IS THOSE WHO ARE WRONG THAT FIGHT FOR CONTROL, INCLUSION, RELIGIOUS LIES, SEXUAL LIES, GENETIC LIES, AND MORE.* Listen, there isn't one God here on Earth therefore, *SOME GODS ARE SPITEFUL; YES, HATE.*

God did not give anyone dominion of Earth, nor did God give dominion to any race to control and manipulate them; the different races.

Some people will tell you God do not like you because; you are Gay, you have different hair, your skin is black, and more. And I refuse to do this because; *MY GOD CANNOT HATE BASED ON SKIN COLOUR, HAIR TYPE, CLEAN SEX, CLEAN LIFE; CLEAN ANYTHING, OR ANYTHING WRONG.* It is us as humans that put ourselves on the Level of God and speak on the behalf of God; well, not on the behalf of My God, but their God in my view.

Their God is their God and Belief, but my God is not spiteful; hate therefore, I write about my God, and teach my Black

Own about our *TRUE AND GOOD GOD THAT IS NOT SPITEFUL; HATE; WHITE BUT BLACK.*

Was this the way I wanted to start this book?

No

I wanted to start it with my dream I had with *the now President of The United States of Death; America; Joe Biden.*

Yes, I cannot fully remember the dream but in the dream; *HE WAS DOING SOMETHING TO BLACK AMERICANS.* I am *not one hundred percent sure* if he issued an *"ELIMINATION ORDER FOR BLACKS." Meaning, he gave the order to KILL BLACK AMERICANS.* However it is, I know something is truly not right with Black Americans, and I will not go back over this. *I told you what this man's agenda was in another book. I also told you what Death wanted in another book and Death got it now.*

Black Americans are not waking up to what's going on around them and, I truly cannot be bothered because; *IF BLACKS TRULY DO NOT UNITE IN A GOOD AND TRUE WAY, WE WILL NEVER BE SAVED FROM WHAT IS TO COME.*

I cannot continue to tell Blacks; *WE ARE THE ELIMINATED RACE GLOBALLY.*

<u>*WE ARE TARGETS FOR THOSE WHO TRULY DO NOT LIKE US.*</u>

<u>*WE ARE TARGETS; THE GAME GLOBALLY FOR THOSE WHO HAVE HIDDEN AGENDAS WHEN IT COMES TO THE DEATH OF BLACK PEOPLE; THE BLACK RACE ON A WHOLE.*</u>

So yes, the kill order must be given shortly.

I cannot with Black People because, <u>*BLACK LANDS ARE NOW PRIME TARGETS FOR THOSE WHO HAVE ALL TO GAIN MONETARILY BECAUSE; CHINESE AND EUROPEAN LANDS HAVE AND HAS DEPLETED THEIR RESOURCES.*</u>

Therefore:

<u>BLACK LANDS FROM AFRICA TO THE CARIBBEAN BETTER WAKE UP BECAUSE SHORTLY.....NO MICHELLE; LEAVE IT ALONE, LEAVE IT ALONE BECAUSE; BLACKS TRULY DO NO PRESERVE THEIR TRUE OWN OR BLACK IDENTITY; WHAT GOD HAS AND HAVE GIVEN THEM; US TO LIVE BY. THEREFORE, THEY; BLACKS DIE AT AND BY THE HANDS OF THEIR ENEMIES LITERALLY.</u>

Earth is changing, and the Devils of Earth did do their job(s). Therefore, Devils preserve Devils. All that is happening now isn't to save humanity, but to save the Select Few. Those devils who are doing all to destroy you.

Their plan is set, and they are living by their plan; yes; their God's Plan which is Death. The Death of You.

Earth lack unity. Therefore, BLACKS GLOBALLY LACK UNITY.

Blacks refuse to unite; come together truthfully to overthrow and conquer all evil here on Earth.

The fate of Black People depend on our true unification.

All evil can be destroyed hence, Blacks have and has truly forgotten about the "POWER AND TRUTH OF ALLELUJAH."

So no, I refuse to worry about Black People because, none can see there is; NO TRUTH OR GOODNESS IN DEATH'S CHILDREN AND PEOPLE.

AS BLACKS, WE CANNOT FASHION OUR LIFE AFTER WHITE PEOPLE.

WE ARE BLACK, AND WE MUST LIVE BLACK.

WE CANNOT WANT OR NEED WHAT WHITE PEOPLE AND THE DIFFERENT RACES HAVE AND HAS. They are not us.

They, the different races have not Black Knowledge apart from the Chinese Race due to Zion; <u>the Chinese Race being apart of Zion.</u>

<u>WE CANNOT CHANGE WHO WE ARE TO PLEASE DEVILS OR THE DEVIL.</u>

WE HAVE TO CHANGE OUR WAY OF LIFE, OUR WAY OF THINKING, THE WAY WE DO THINGS TRUTHFULLY AND RIGHT FOR THE BETTER GOOD OF SELF, AND OUR RACE.

WE CAN NO LONGER LET THE DIFFERENT RACES PICKY BACK OFF US WHILE THEY ARE BUILDING THEMSELVES, THEIR NATIONS, AND WE AS BLACK PEOPLE ARE STILL POOR, OUR LAND AND LANDS ARE STILL POOR AS WELL AS, FOREIGN OWNED.

AS BLACKS, <u>WE CAN NO LONGER BE INDEBTED TO DEATH WHEN WE CAN PAY OFF OUR DEBT TO DEATH IF WE COME TOGETHER COLLECTIVELY AND TRUE.</u> THUS, TRUE UNIFICATION IS A MUST FOR

THOSE WHO ARE OF GOOD AND TRUE LIFE; BLACK LIFE.

We cannot say; "BLACK LIVES MATTER," AND CONTINUE TO KILL OURSELVES.

We cannot say; "BLACK LIVES MATTER," AND CONTINUE TO FIGHT WITH EACH OTHER, AND KILL EACH OTHER.

We cannot say; "BLACK LIVES MATTER," and not:
Think Black
Be Black
Live Black
Educate us the Black Way
Have our *"OWN BLACK GOD,"* and more.

We cannot say; "BLACK LIVES MATTER," and not buy Black.

We cannot say; "BLACK LIVES MATTER," and not know "Allelujah; Lovey and God."

We cannot say; "BLACK LIVES MATTER," and not respect each other.

We cannot say; "BLACK LIVES MATTER," and not *BUILD US; BLACKS GOOD AND TRUE.*

Yes, there is more but I will leave it at that for now.

WE AS BLACK PEOPLE HAVE TO SERVE OUR PURPOSE IN LIFE FOR SELF AND PEOPLE; OUR OWN BLACK NATIONS.

WE CAN NO LONGER LIVE POOR AND DESITUTE.

We can no longer live hand to mouth.
We can no longer live door to door. Nomads
We have to live settled.
We have to preserve us.
We have to live right and true for us.
We have to find our true place in life.

We have to regain the trust of our Black God. Therefore, we have to find our own Black God good and true.

We cannot continue to live in Biblical Lies.

Black Nations have tremendous resources yet, Black Nations have and has become lap dogs; beggars for the different Global Corporate Greed, the IMF, Europeans, Chinese, and more.

It is so cool right now.

Did I dream me being in the hospital?

Yes, but I am not going to worry about that dream, I just have to take better control of me and my health. Right now, my health need major improvement as I am getting more headaches and I truly cannot have this.

As for the Rap Industry. I did dream about this industry, but I cannot tell you which artists are going to be feuding. I so cannot remember the dream.

Therefore, I will not worry about anyone in the Music Industry and or, Entertainment Industry because; *they are satan Owned.* Death owns them due to the pact and pacts many have and has made with the devil for fame and money. *Many and or, all did not think about their Spiritual Life that once you SELL YOUR SOUL TO THE DEVIL, THAT SELLING IS IRREVOCABLE. SATAN AND OR, THE DEVIL OWN YOU, YOUR FINANCIAL ASSETS, YOUR WIFE OR HUSBAND, YOUR CHILDREN, YOUR OTHER PARTNERS IF YOU HAVE OUTSIDE PARTNERS, AND MORE.*

Absolutely none in the Music and or, Entertainment Industry can or will escape hell; their hell with Death and the Demons of Hell.

Time is winding down for humans here on Earth. *SPIRITUAL DEATH MUST COME TO EARTH AND SPIRITUAL DEATH IS ON ITS WAY.*

All those spirits; souls that have died that has and have their name in the Book of Death, Death must now start taking to Hell.

That one day for Death is up therefore, billions are on the Docket of Death literally.

Sorry everyone, it's July 8, 2021, and I did not say a good and blessed morning to you all. Truly forgive me, and a blessed and good morning to all of you.

Did I dream about my second child, his friend Binky, and me?

Yes. I had purchased a Blue Jacket and I was modelling it for them. So do not know what that dream means but I am leaving it alone.

My body need heat because the cool breeze is coming into my room as I have my window fully open, and the cold breeze is playing havoc on my body especially my leg muscles.

I am so going back to bed and going under the sheet.

Michelle

It's July 9, 2021, and I did dream about the Canadian Prime Minister Justin Trudeau. Wow because the dream had to do with these White Women and his father.

I did not see his father in the dream, but Pierre Elliot Trudeau was apart of the dream. I was talking about his no nonsense ways, and I am so going to leave things alone.

Canada has shifted; moved away from the direction it was to take. And no, I will not get involved in Canadian Politics because in my view; CANADA WILL FOREVER USE FIRST NATIONS PEOPLE AS THEIR SCAPEGOATS. And I am going to go further because in my view; the NEW GOVERNOR GENERAL THAT WAS APPOINTED IS NOTHING BUT A JOKE AND SLAP IN THE FACE TO INDIGENOUS PEOPLE OF CANADA. YES, THE PUPPET ON A STRING FOR WHITES.

Yes, you can hate me for this, BUT TO ME SHE WAS ONLY APPOINTED BECAUSE OF THE SCANDAL; ROMAN CATHOLIC SCANDAL AND WHAT WHITES DID TO INDIGENOUS PEOPLE HERE ON CANADA TO TRY TO HIDE THEIR; WHITE PEOPLE'S SHAME AND GUILT.

For me, and to me; *White People will always do all to hide their shame and guilt by buying their way out of things and covering up their ills like nothing happened.*

For me, I would have never accepted that appointment.

What Whites have done and are still doing to First Nations People here in Canada is truly not right.

To me and for me. What this new appointment; new Governor General has done by accepting this post is say; *"it's okay. I forgive you for all the ills Canadian and or, Whites have and has done to First Nation People. I accept your guilt offering therefore saving you – Whites from your Sin and Sins; Guilt and Ills done unto First Nation People and or, Indigenous Canadians."*

THEREFORE, WHITES WILL ALWAYS DO ALL TO BUY THEIR WAY OUT OF HELL BECAUSE; THE DIFFERENT NATIONS THEY'VE DONE WRONGS; ILLS TO AND OR, UNTO WILLINGLY LET THEM GET AWAY WITH IT. *Thus, many accept their Guilt, and Measly Blood; Death Offerings.*

Now tell me. Is your dead loved ones back from the grave and living with you in the flesh?

Are they; your dead loved ones not still suffering; still in pain in the grave?

Are you still not grieving for your loved ones, and true loved ones?

So now tell me. *Why allow Whites to PAY YOU FOR DEATH; KILLING YOUR LOVED ONES, TRUE FAMILY MEMBERS AND GET AWAY WITH IT?*

Why the Bleep don't the Governments of the Globe; Earth step in and, *SHUT DOWN EVERY ROMAN CATHOLIC CHURCH AND SCHOOL INCLUDING, CEMETERIES IN CANADA, AND GLOBALLY?*

Why condone murder by this church and the different churches?

No, when did God; the TRUE AND LIVING GOD become Death, and the target practice for those who hate life, and lie on life; God?

When did God; the TRUE AND LIVING GOD ordain Pedophiles, and Murderers to oversee any one or any race here on Earth?

Therefore, Devils; Demons use, and prey on people and their vulnerability with the use of God's name, and their so-called religious ordinances; lies.

As humans we need to stop letting our different Government Officials, Corporate Greed, Pharmaceutical Greed, Religious Greed, Gang – Drug Greed, and more use us as scapegoats in the ills they do here on Earth for profit, and prophet.

DUTTY CAANE COME CLEAN, AND THE ROMAN CATHOLIC CHURCH IS NOT CLEAN. THUS, THE PEODPHILES AND MURDERERS OF THE ROMAN CATHOLIC CHURCH. THUS, THE WHITE RACE WILL ALWAYS USE GOD AS A PASS TO GET AWAY WITH THEIR ATROCITIES; MURDERS THEY COMMIT; DO HERE ON EARTH.

No, I am SICK AND TIRED OF WHITE DEVILS HIDING BEHIND RELIGION TO CARRY OUT THEIR ANUS ACTS OF ABUSE AND MURDER.

No Lovey man, *HUMANS NEED TO TRULY WAKE UP AND TAKE BACK THEIR LIFE. WHITES SHOULD NOT GET AWAY WITH THEIR WRONGS.*

Yes, I know I should not interfere but I am. *I am still hurt BECAUSE OF HER LIE.* It got too far when it comes to me Lovey come on now. I prayed to you for years to take me out of this land, and it has and have come to this; *HER LIE. NOW TELL ME, HOW FAIR AND TRUE ARE YOU TO ME LOVEY?*

How just and fair are you to me Life Wise, and you Lovey Wise here on Earth?

Now tell me, IN ALL I'VE PRAYED TO YOU FOR AND YOU'VE IGNORNED ME, DO YOU NOT CONDONE THE LIE SHE TOLD ON ME AND MY DOG?

ARE YOU NOT A WILLING PARTICIPANT TO THIS; HER LIE LOVEY?

IT HAPPENED TO YOU LOVEY WITH RELIGION.

NOW IT HAPPENED TO ME AND MY DOG. Her lie did get to me because; I mainly walk my dog. There are days I cannot walk her due to health, the cold, and me being at my dad's but, I am her primary walker. Plus, I know my dog.

Now tell me; <u>HOW FAR AND HOW MUCH LONGER ARE YOU GOING TO LET WHITES GET AWAY WITH THEIR WRONGS HERE ON EARTH AND IN THE SPIRITUAL REALM INCLUDING UNIVERSE?</u>

<u>How long must White People get away with their wrongs; evils?</u>

<u>How much longer should White People; White Devils no matter the race or skin colour rule Earth?</u>

WHITES CANNOT HIDE BEHIND RELGION ANYMORE LOVEY COME ON NOW.

Now let me ask you this Lovey just to be racist, and truly forgive me but:

<u>"HOW MANY WORLD WARS DID BLACK PEOPLE START?"</u>

<u>"HOW MANY BIBLES OF LIES AND NASTINESS DID BLACK PEOPLE WRITE ABOUT YOU AND LIFE LOVEY?"</u>

"HOW MANY SCROLLS OF LIES DO BLACK PEOPLE; BLACK NATIONS CLAIM TO HAVE LOVEY?"

"HOW MUCH STRIFE DO BLACK PEOPLE CREATE WITH THE DIFFERENT NATIONS?"

Now tell me. *"DID MANY EUROPEAN WHITES NOT GO INTO AFRICA AND MASSACRE MANY AFRICANS WITHOUT A CAUSE DUE TO GREED?"*

And Black People put it together with Massa and Mass from the word Massacre.

"ARE BLACK PEOPLE NOT THEIR; WHITES PRIMARY TARGETS WHEN IT COMES TO KILLING BLACKS VIA THEIR MANUFACTURED DRUGS, VIRUSES, AND DISEASES?"

"HOW MANY BLACK EUROPEANS DID WHITES SLAUGHTER HENCE, THEIR BLACK PLAGUE?"

I know the cause of Slavery but, for the sake of Slavery despite me knowing the truth of Slavery. *"HOW*

MANY BLACKS DID WHITES RAPE AND MURDER; SLAUGHTER ON THEIR WAY TO THE DIFFERENT LANDS, AND IN THE DIFFERENT LANDS?"

So now tell me. "WHAT GOODNESS AND TRUTH IS THEIR IN WHITES, AND WHITE HISTORY?"

Do they; Whites even have shame and guilt?

THEREFORE, YOU LOVEY CANNOT LET THIS VILE RACE OF BEINGS CONTINUE TO GET AWAY WITH THEIR WRONGS; ILLS THEY'VE DONE TO ROB PEOPLE OF THEIR LAND, LIFE, AND RIGHTS HERE ON EARTH.

HOW FAIR AND JUST ARE YOU RIGHT NOW?

Does Life; Good and True Life not matter to you Lovey?

You know my pain of being in this land. NOW ONE HAS AND HAVE TOLD A CATEGORICAL LIE ON ME AND MY DOG.

So yes, in many ways, I do blame you for this lie because; IF YOU HAD LISTENED TO MY TRUTH

AND TRULY PROVIDED FOR ME, THEN THIS LIE WOULD HAVE NEVER HAPPENED IN MY VIEW.

IF YOU HAD TRULY LOVED ME AND NOT LOVE SO, I WOULD HAVE BEEN FREE FROM HER LIE AND BE IN THE RIGHT ENVIRONMENT; YOU AND ME. And yes, despite my talk; I am doing all to prey on your sympathetic side of truth.

So no, it's hard for me right now. You know my situation and you would rather see me unhappy, lied upon as well as, see me dead in a land and place I truly do not want or need to be in. I prayed to you true, talked to you true, and in my praying and talking, you've ignored me; abandoned me; why?

So no, why should I continue to trust you.

Yes, my life is not straight to the way I want and need it to be, but for God's sake; do not lie on me and my dog like that man.

How do you live with yourself?

No Lovey, it's painful thus, *I know how you feel when humans go to church and lie on you.*

It's painful thus, I know your hurt and pain and now I am adding more hurt and pain to you with my hurt and pain, and I shouldn't. I should not let her lie affect me because;

it's my dog she truly lied on, and not me. I get it Lovey, but I can't.

I truly can't.

I want and need to run away from this land, and I know I will get over therefore, please for my sake, truly do not continue to hold me hostage in a land where I am truly not happy or comfortable in.

Truly do not continue to hold me hostage; captive in a land where someone has and have categorically lied on my dog, and yes, me because; I am the primary walker for my dog.

I can't deal with it. Therefore, I cannot save Canada for you. Yes, I will give you your plant and or, seed happily, *but I will never forget or forgive this lie of her because; it is still truly affecting me.* *Now, it's spilt over into my relationship with you.*

No Lovey, truly find someone else in GOODNESS AND IN TRUTH TO SAVE CANADA FOR YOU BECAUSE I TRULY CANNOT.

I just want to be far away from this land in my own world and realm now. I don't even want to think about you right now Lovey. I am hurt. I can't be you because I know you too are hurt.

No, we are humans, and we do Sin, I am not exception, but don't look at me and lie to me like that to my face come on now.

Maybe I am taking it overboard, but I truly do not think so.

No Lovey, you are my saviour, but; *why were you not my saviour with her?*

So no, *I step aside from Canada literally.* Do what you need to do with Canada but, *truly do it without me.*

Like I said, I will plant your seed and or, plant and or, tree here because this you require of me truthfully, but as far me staying here in Canada, *I will not stay in this land.*

If I have to disobey you; then so be it. Truth is my good and true stay and gain, and I cannot stay with someone; a God that continually hurt me need wise, pain wise, people wise, health wise, and more.

Yes, many things you've protected me from over the years and I truly thank you for this, but I cannot continue my journey with you Canada Wise.

It's time for me to truly sever all ties with this land and do all to save me in another land without you. Yes, you can be hurt but, I need to do this. I need to let you go because of hurt and pain. I know I am hurting you, but Lovey, you know me when it comes to my life and you, the land I am living in, what I write, my truth, and more.

I have to stay true to me.

I have to live with me.

I have to be me good and true. Please just live your life because I am stepping away from you.

Yes, you've done a lot for me.

You saved me, but now you cannot save me.

You could not save me from her lie.
You could not protect me from her lie.

Yes, maybe I put too much on you and for this I am truly sorry, but I have to step aside from you.

I need to heal me. *And no, I am not giving up on our true relationship.* I just have to get over and find me due to her lie. But in truth, truly find someone to save Canada for you. I will not save this land in goodness and in truth, nor will I save anyone wicked and evil, and you know this.

Please do not be angry with me, but truly forgive me, but I have to be truly me. You know me when it comes to people who hurt me. I truly don't want to be in the same place as them, and if I can move to another universe where they that hurt me truly cannot find me, I would build that universe and go there just to be away from people, and the negatives of this world.

My tummy is hungry, and I need to find something to eat but I feel for nothing. I need to get onto a vegan diet where I incorporate more vegetables in my life.

So Lovey, despite my pain, truly be you and continue to be the good and true you, you are.

No Lovey, the seed and or, tree and or, plant I plant for you in Canada, it truly cannot save Canadians, White People Globally or any North American Land or Lands. I truly don't want it to on this day. And no, I am not taking your truth from you Lovey. Many things you do not listen to me on. Therefore, do you good and true for Canada.

I will not take away your right to save this land. However, this plant, seed, or tree cannot save any form of Evil or Negative Forces; Energy or People anywhere. Evil and Negative Forces cannot be saved Lovey come on now.

I would not say I am selfish, but I need the lies, deceit, ills, abuse of every race here on Earth to be shut down. I can't live in lies anymore Lovey come on now.

I can't live in Sin and amongst Sin anymore.

I need good and true life and I cannot have good and true life here on Earth amongst all the negatives of Life and Spirit; the Spiritual Realm.

I did get an afternoon nap and I dreamt Wayne Lonesome. We were at a party, and he was with these *THREE BLACK GENTLEMAN.*

I said you are Wayne Lonesome, and he agreed. Acknowledging him we began to walk and talk. On his face you could see gray hair stubbles. It did not look like him, but it was him.

In the dream it seemed as if he was scared.

It was as if he was getting death threats.

We also talked about the internet. And yes, I am forgetting some little things that I cannot remember like if he wanted and or, we had a relationship.

So not going to analyze this dream because; *JAMAICA IS TRULY NOT WHAT IT SEEMS. THE DEMONS ARE LET LOOSE IN JAMAICA THEREFORE, DEATH WALK ON LAND AND IS TAKING AT WILL.*

I am so hungry right now that my stomach is in a uproar hunger wise. Just thinking of food makes me sick to my stomach.

My body cannot tolerate certain foods right now to the point of wanting to vomit when I eat certain foods.

Just this afternoon due to hunger, I made macaroni and cheese with two boiled eggs, and the gag factor. I so wanted to vomit.

My body is changing where it doesn't want or need meat. This is good for me. There are times when my body go into vegetable mode but unfortunately, *cooking is so not my strong suit these days.* Body gets too weak due to hunger which is my fault. I do take too long to eat, nor do I truly want to eat any and anything.

I have sardines but my body truly cannot stand sardines. Fast food is just disgusting for me right now. Man, I wish I had my own Jamaican Chef to cook me all I need right now.

Maybe one day I will meet my wonderful and clean Jamaican Guy that can cook and treat me right.

Michelle

Though this book is called _RACIST OR NOT_, I truly do not know if this is book racist. I did let loose in _CHANGES_ racist wise so forgive me if this book is not what it is supposed to be.

These are what I put on paper before I wrote what you read above.

Do enjoy, and if you can spread the knowledge and message of these books via your Instagram Account, Twitter, Face Book Account, and or, the different Social Media Outlets you have and use, I would greatly appreciate it.

Listen, I do exist. I am not a robot.

I am old fashioned in that; all I want to do is, write and plant. Finding an agent for me is like finding a needle in a haystack. I cannot follow guidelines of submitting this or that to them; an agent and or, publicist; thus, the dinosaur and or, Whale of Old in me. It's hard so, if you can help me to promote these books, please do so in a good and true way.

So, here we go with what I put on paper.

Michelle

It's a new day July 1st, Canada Day, and a holiday.

Walked my dog
Had breakfast
Played my game

Now, I want something to do
Yes, the mind is in a different zone

Damn, does it ever want to be naked on a beach.

Yes, on my back getting my belly and boobs tanned.

Don't laugh
Mind takes me places
Yes, exotic places

Hey, can you fancy me

Writing erotica
Well, erotica my way and not the sleezy way.

I am so not going to say it's a dancehall thing either.

But wow to dance – the dance in Dancehall.

Steamy
Erotic
Way too sexual

Damn
That's all I got to say.

Michelle

Listen, I am not going to bash Dancehall. Jamaican Females will forever be X-rated.

Some have no issues being scantly clothed before people. I have an issue with this.

Now, *ELEPHANT MAN.* I am going to bash you.

I know you don't care but I care.

DANCE APPROPRIATION

Yes, you are a DJ and Dancer, but I am calling you out for *DANCE APPROPRIATION* in your Official Video for *"CAN'T STOP DANCING."*

No, I truly love Black Dance, but when I see you promoting WHITE FEMALES SHOWING UP BLACK DANCEHALL MOVES, I have an issue with you. Yes, you have Black Dancers in your video, BUT DANCEHALL QUEENS TO ME SHOULD BE PROMOTED AND DANCED BY BLACKS.

All too often Whites CAPITALIZE ON WHAT WE AS BLACK PEOPLE TEACH THEM. WHAT THEY LEARN FROM US AND DO NOT GIVE BLACKS CREDIT FOR TEACHING THEM.

If Whites were fair on this level to Blacks; then yes, I would have no issues with WHITE DANCEHALL QUEENS, BUT THEY DO NOT GIVE BLACKS CREDIT THEREFORE, I HAVE AN ISSUE WITH WHITES CAPITALIZING OFF BLACK PEOPLE.

Michelle
July 1, 2021

Medically Blacks do not get credit for our inventions.

Scientifically Blacks do not get credit.

CEO Wise, Blacks do not get credit and, many Blacks run some of the biggest corporations globally that are not Black Owned.

Musically, we do not get credit for our Music. And please do not go there with the BET bullshit. BET is not Black Owned and was never Black Owned.

True Black don't sell out Blacks.
True Blacks keep Blacks informed.
True Blacks ride out the wave.
True Blacks sell to Blacks.

Diversity you are saying.

Listen to me now.

DIVERSITY JUSTIFIES THE WEAK; GREEDY.

DIVERSITY JUSTIFY THOSE WHO HAVE A LOT TO LOSE AND GAIN OFF YOU. Meaning, if
they don't sell diversity, they lose financially – profit wise.

SO:
Diversity is Corporate owned – Money for those who have a lot to lose financially.

When Whites are murdering Blacks, who's claiming diversity?

How many Whites stand up for Blacks and cry foul; *STOP BEING UNJUST TO BLACKS?*

So, diversity to me and for me is bullshit. When has Whites ever truly liked Blacks unless *THEFT AND MONEY is involved; all they have to gain off, and on the BACKS OF BLACKS?*

Michelle
July 01, 2021

Yes, you can say Racism on my part, but I have to be the good and true me and tell you as it is; yes, how I feel.

I can be, and I am a very nice person but, the way Blacks are treated globally especially in European Lands irks me then to have them; European Whites acting Black by dancing Black.

Yes, we as Black People are to be blamed because; *"WE EMBRACE EVERYONE."*

When they see colour many of us do not.

Like I said, if Blacks were credited by Whites and yes, compensated then no, I would have no issues with this, *but Whites do not credit Black People for the things we do.* Instead, they take Ownership of all Blacks have and has done.

They distort Black Life.
Lie on Black Life.
Gain; profit off Black Life.

Say it so I can blast you.

How many of you rock Black Designer shoes, clothing?

Read Black Books.
Rock your natural hair.

Rock your natural skin without the god-awful crap you call make up, the hideous tattoos, the skin bleaching therefore, you depriving you psychologically of your self worth, and more.

Michelle
July (01) 2021

So yes, we as Blacks are our own worst nightmare. <u>*WE DEPRIVE OUR SELF OF OUR BLACKNESS.*</u>

<u>*We deprive our self of our Black Worth.*</u>

<u>*We deprive our self of our own Black God.*</u>

<u>*We devalue our self.*</u>

<u>*We refuse to build Black by uniting truthfully.*</u>

<u>*We refuse to build true Black Wealth that not only support you but, support the Black Race on a whole.*</u>

Many Blacks when they have, they look down on other Blacks.

Glorify their wealth.

Yes, I will not knock you. It took you robbing yourself of your soul to get it. Therefore, no one should be jealous of any of you.

I myself refuse to lose my soul to gain it all financially.

I know hell therefore, it's a foolish man, woman, and child that would sacrifice their life here on Earth to die a brutal death Spiritually.

Therefore, Blacks need to change how we live.
How we speak to each other.

How we communicate with each other.

We need to change our language. And no, truly not to Ebonics.

We need to change the way we dress.
How we do business at home and internationally.

We need to change the way we eat.

We have to; must do all to cut out the Junk Food, and start eating naturally organic – healthy.

And no, Certified Organic is not Organic; 100% Pesticide Free.

Genetically Modified foods in not organic; original.
As Blacks, we have to start owning fully; Black Brands.

We as Black People need our own Internet Platforms independent of:

Face Book
Google
Twitter
Tik Tok
Snap Chat
Instagram, and more.

We need true Black Networks.
We need to have true Black Goals.
We need to regain our True Black Self.

Our Black Rights.

Our Black God.
Our Black Knowledge.
Our Black way of doing things.
Our Black Family, and more.

Michelle
July (01) 2021

Yes, go ahead and call me racist and say; God don't like you.

God could never have chosen you.

God loves everyone, and I am spiteful and hateful, and I am going to petition your books to be banned.

And I say; go right ahead. Petition my books to be banned. *I want and need you to.*

1. I know God and Death so go right ahead.

2. I never ever said, I am the Chosen. I've been open and true by telling you "*God told me to write a book.*" and, I've written many. Plus, the book God required of me, God got. *Thus, THE NEW BOOK OF KNOWLEDGE AS WRITTEN BY MICHELLE AND LOVEY: GOD.*

   So yes, Life has the Book of Life: Knowledge, and Death has the Book of Death. Your so-called Holy Bible.

3. No, God can't like me. God truly loves me. Therefore, I know I have a place in God's World and Realm. Can you say the same?

4. God is not for everyone because different people; races, have different gods.

And no, you cannot speak for God because; *my God is Black. THE TRUE AND LIVING GOD THAT*

CREATED IT ALL GOOD AND TRUE. Thus, the Language of God only a select few here on Earth has; can write; use. And no, this language is not Hebrew, Yiddish and or, Gibberish, nor is it Arabic.

So yes, God has a language and Death well, the Demons of Hell have their language thus, the gibberish some speak whilst Speaking in Tongues. Yes, their way of communicating with the dead; Demons literally.

So go ahead; speak so that my Black God, my Bunnununus can shut you the hell up, and down.

Michelle
July 2021

So yes, Racism please those who have absolutely no truth in them.

Racism suits those who want to suppress the truth.

Racism suits those who cannot speak the truth. They hide their feelings no matter how it hurts. Thus, Closeted Racists.

I refuse to hide my truth and feelings from anyone. You don't have to like me. This is your given and right.

Yes, you can speak on the behalf of your God; but truly do not speak on the behalf of mine; my God because, you truly do not know my God, what my God is worth, what my God can do, and more.

Your God hath no worth; value hence your so-called Holy Bible of Filth and Nastiness.

You live nasty therefore, you are going to die nasty.

Your God is Death. My God is Life; *THE TRUE AND LIVING GOD.*

Michelle
July 2021

My bubbies are so huge, they fell like 50 – 100 pounds right now.

So have to design clothes for the full-figured women my way. I truly need comfort my way Clothing Wise.

I do not know why I feel as if my assets; breasts have and has gotten bigger.

Truly love my breasts yes, but hate; truly loathe my lover back pain.

And no, I refuse to go under the knife to get a breast reduction.

I wanted bigger breasts, prayed for them hence; *I am a NATURAL CHESTY PERSON.*

Nope, can't give up my assets. Just need to find. Nope.

Yes, the right person who will truly love all of me including my personality.

Michelle
July 02, 2021

Oh lord my mind is going there but I can't go there. Truly don't want or need to.

Too X-rated what my mind is thinking, and I need to keep it clean on this day.

Vibe not right in that way.

Hair is unruly right now. It's grown and now I need a braid up; someone to cornrow my hair neatly and perfectly but; I truly do not allow people in my hair in that way.

Yes, I have family members that are hairdressers, and I don't really go to them.

Yes, I want to go totally bald, but my mind is screaming no.

Yes, I am bored of my hair because; *I am the laziest person maintenance wise.*

How about you?
Are you lazy like me hair wise?
Do you maintain your hair?

How do you care for your hair?
Do you cut your hair often?
Do you like long hair?
Do you prefer short hair?
Does your hair grow fast?

Let me know.

Michelle
July 02, 2021

We say Money is the root of all evil but I say; *it's the people behind the money that are the root of all evil.* Thus, many who are wealthy had to obtain their wealth the evil – Sinful Way.

In order to gain substantial wealth, you have to sell your soul.

You have to live and die by Death; *the Abrahamic Code of Law and Laws.*

Thus, Americans have to pledge allegiance to Death. It is their law therefore, America is the Land of Death; the Dead. So, Blacks see them and know them.

Americans cannot live by Life; they have to; must live by Death.

Americans have to feed Death.

Thus, their Mounting and Staggering Debt with Death. See their war machines, the different armies; people they employ to kill; actively murder others in different nations. No, America alone is not guilty thus; *only 10% OF HUMANS WILL BE SAVED WHEN ALL IS SAID AND DONE.*

Michelle
July 03, 2021

And that was all I wrote on paper. As for my mood today July 11, 2021, I am not sure what to call it. Not in a rut but my body is weak – draining energy wise.

Had a coffee and some crackers but that cannot sustain and maintain my body.

Did I dream about God this morning?

Yes

I cannot remember the full extent of the dream apart from God answering and or, blessing someone in my family. I can't remember if it was my last child or my sister, but God was answering them and or, blessing them with their desire; that which they asked God for.

This is truly great for me, and I don't want to distort anything, but I am going to.

I don't know. No, I do know. This morning whilst in my washroom washing my face and brushing my teeth, I was saying to myself and yes, you can say God that; *I would never ever forgive God for keeping me in Canada.*

My true and good desire is not this land, and I cannot comprehend why God would keep me prisoner here. I truly do not want or need my body when my spirit shed the flesh to be housed in this land.

God know this, yet God is keeping me truly trapped in a land I truly, honestly, and wholeheartedly do not want or need to be in.

Yes, I talk about this a lot but there is absolutely no forgiveness for me with God in keeping me in a land I more than categorically truthfully and truly do not want or need to be in.

I just can't anymore.

Now I have to wonder why my mother took me out of Jamaica. Yes, I don't blame her for her efforts and yes, *God did deem Jamaica unclean.*

God has and have been protecting me from going into Jamaica due to the land being unclean.

Because God has and have deemed Jamaica unclean, I am forbidden to step foot in that land.

To disobey God is my death spiritually. So, if God has forbidden you from doing certain things, you have to obey God and stay your ground. The day you disobey God, is the day your name is taken from the Book of Life and put into the Book of Death.

Therefore, when the spirit leaves the flesh; body, you *"AUTOMATICALLY GO TO HELL AND WOE – TRULY WOE BE UNTO YOU."* Trust me, your beating wow; I truly do not want to see.

So, because Man say God gave us laws, and these laws were put in man's so-called holy bible, and humans disobey the Laws of God then; billions have their name in the Book of

Death due to disobedience; disobeying the Law and Laws of God.

Listen, I truly do not blame my Mother or God for this move; taking me from my land of birth, but I am truly not happy here and will never ever be truly happy here. This, God cannot see. Therefore, I feel like a captive here in this land.

Right now, my hurt and pain outweigh any goodness God has and have done for me here in this land.

I know I should not say that, but this is the way I truly feel right now. Give me the resources I need to do the good and truth you need me to do so that I can truly leave out of this land in goodness and in truth.

Where is my true happiness in all of this?

Where is my life's worth in all of this?

Yes, I know my life's worth is in me and God but; I truly do not feel it is on this day. I feel abandoned God Wise.

Yes, I want and need out and would hope that God would want and need a true and better way out for me.

Maybe I am clouded this morning and I cannot see the bigger and better picture of what God truly need and want for me. But, I just want out. I want to be planting somewhere where I can find true happiness by the water; river or sea with God.

I need to plant Cherry Trees, Apple Trees, Pear Trees, Breadfruit Trees, Lime Trees, Banana, Mango Trees, all that is good and true I so truly more than eternally need to plant in goodness and in truth. Oh God how I desire and crave this with God and Mother Earth, and neither God or Mother Earth can see my goodness and truth with them.

Oh my God how I truly want and need to plant good and true with true love and care and I cannot have this because; *GOD IS TAKING MY GOODNESS AND TRUTH FROM ME IN THIS WAY.*

I truly do not want or need to plant here because here; the land I am in is truly not my good and true heart's desire. Hopefully one day God would feel me, and hear me and yes, cry and say; *Michelle I am sorry for keeping you against your will in a land you truly, truly, truly, do not desire to be in.* Here you go; I have come truthfully with Mother Earth and have chosen this spot for you and our good and true own. Build good and true here because; you are good and true to me in your heart, and all that you do for me.

Truly forgive me for going against your good and true will.

Truly hopefully everyone, truly hopefully because; I am truly hurt right now.

Yes, there is more that I want to say but don't know what to say.

Michelle

If I could say pain, pain go away never come back again, never inflame by body, mind, and spirit again ever, knowing my pain would leave forever ever and never return, I would in an instant.

I truly do not know why my body is so up and down pain wise. Yesterday July 11, 2021, my lower back pain got so bad that I wanted to cry. I don't know if it's the bra I am wearing but God to the amount of pain that I was in. I had to call my son; last child to help me in bed. I truly hate days like these.

I so need a permanent solution to this because I truly cannot live like this for the rest of my life. The hardest part for me at times in not getting....never mind because I know I am not in the right environment period.

Once travel is opened up truthfully and, _YOUR FUNDAMENTAL HUMAN RIGHTS IS NOT TAKEN FROM YOU VACCINE WISE, I WILL TRAVEL TO SOMEPLACE WARM._

No, this bullshit is truly getting to me now with _WHITE PEOPLE AND THEIR BLEEPING DECEIT AND LIES, AND LOVEY IS TRULY NOT WALKING AWAY FROM THIS DEMONIC RACE OF MURDERERS. Nor is Mother Earth doing anything in my view to shut these demons down._

I should not have to travel from land to land by taking your vaccines of Death that includes tracking devices. I have a right to life.

<u>*Why the Bleep don't your Satanic Race stop developing and making viruses that you infect and kill people with?*</u>

<u>*Bunch of Bleeping Murderers that have no worth or self worth in life thus, your "DEATH RECORD GLOBALLY."*</u>

No, I am pissed off at Lovey right now.

When I want to do wrong, you see how quickly I am being warned yet; <u>*WHEN IT COMES TO MY HAPPINESS, MY FUNDAMENTAL HUMAN RIGHTS, MY LIFE, MY LIVING GOOD AND CLEAN, AND MORE GOOD AND TRUE THINGS, I AM BEING IGNORED BY LOVEY.*</u> *Yet, the White Race of Demons get away with all their ills daily.*

No Lovey is truly not fair to me in this way.

No, today it is not about being spoiled. <u>*THE ILLS OF MAN AND MEN HAVE TO STOP. I AM FED UP OF WHITE PEOPLE MALICIOUSLY, WILLINGLY, AND KNOWINGLY TAKING MY*</u>

FUNDAMENTAL HUMAN RIGHTS FROM ME WITH THEIR SICK; DISEASED BULLSHIT THEY MANUFACTURE IN LABORATORIES TO KILL.

"THE WHITE RACE FEED DEATH PERIOD." So now tell me. WHERE IS GOOD AND TRUE LIFE HERE ON EARTH?

IT'S BAD ENOUGH THAT I HAVE TO LIVE AMONGST THESE DEMONS OF THE WORST KIND AND NOTHING IS BEING DONE ABOUT THEM HERE ON EARTH, AND IN THE SPIRITUAL REALM.

I AM FED UP NOW.

NO ONE SHOULD HAVE TO LIVE BY DEATH; THE DEATH WAY COME ON NOW.

No, God and Lovey to me is not worth it right now to the way I feel and yes, my anger. You are not with me, nor do you truly love me come on now.

WHY THE HELL SHOULD I HAVE TO TAKE YOUR STINKING DUTTY VACCINE? THAT WHICH YOU MADE IN A LAB TO INFECT PEOPLE WITH YOUR DAMN COVID-19 BULLSHIT, AND MORE.

No Lovey. People need to look into how much of this virus; Covid-19 Virus they pit in their vaccines. Thus, it's people from developed nations that go to other lands and infect others without knowing it.

No Lovey, <u>why is it all is not taken from Diseased Scientists?</u>

<u>Why is Death protecting them; Diseased Scientists here on Earth, and in the Spiritual Realm?</u>

No Lovey. How sick can you be to knowingly, and willingly develop diseases and viruses to kill?

Have you no heart or remorse?

No, that was a stupid question Michelle. Demons have no heart. Death have no heart therefore, no Life is with them; just Death.

<u>WHY THE HELL SHOULD I ALLOW YOU TO TRAP AND TRACK ME?</u>

<u>WEY UNNU GUH TRACK UNNU MUMMA!!!!!!!!!!!!</u>

<u>I am not your child. You are not responsible for me; my parents and God is responsible for me.</u>

<u>How dare the lots of you violate "MY FUNDAMENTAL HUMAN RIGHTS AND</u>

GOD GIVEN HUMAN RIGHTS" HERE ON EARTH!!!!!!!!

NO, YOU AS PHARMACEUTICALS CORPORTATIONS; GREED; CORPORATE GREED, AND GOVERNMENT OFFICIALS; LITERAL DEMONS ARE NOT MY BLEEPING PARENTS. I SHOULD NOT HAVE TO LIVE ACCORDING TO YOUR LIES; MURDEROUS WAYS.

YOU'RE ALL A BUNCH OF JUDAS. Thus, the _"SELLING OF DEATH GLOBALLY."_

No to the way I feel right now. _MOTHER EARTH AND GOD ARE BITCH NIGGERS TO MY ANGER._

NO, IF I HAD THE SAY SO AND KNOWLEDGE, NO EVIL WOULD BE HERE ON EARTH TO BOTHER THE GOOD AND TRUE OR KILL ANY FORM OF GOOD AND TRUE LIFE. Trust me, all would be gone literally.

I am so sick and tired of the way Earth is being run by _DEMONS THAT LIVE TO KILL AND DO KILL._

I AM FED UP OF GOD AND THE LIES OF GOD BECAUSE IF LOVEY; GOD WAS TRULY

TRUE, LOVEY WOULD SHOW ME WHAT TO DO TO SHUT ALL FACETS OF EVIL DOWN HERE ON EARTH RIGHT AWAY. BUT, BECAUSE LOVEY LOVE FI SI MI SUFFA.....let is go Michelle because Lovey knows all my suffering here on Earth I will not forgive.

All the evils that the different race has and have done here on Earth THERE IS ABSOLUTELY NO FORGIVENESS IN MY BOOK AND WORLD FOR THEM.

And yes, I know; I am not the forgiver of Life and Death. Those who you have erred are the ones to forgive you. But if I could and was a forgiver. CATEGORICALLY WITHOUT END, NO FORGIVENESS FOR WICKED AND EVIL PEOPLE; SINFUL DOERS THAT WILLING GO OUT OF THEIR WAY TO LIE, DECEIVE, AND KILL.

Trust me, if Mother Earth listen to me...no forget it because, MY ANGER IS GETTING THE BEST OF ME THIS MORNING DUE TO PAIN. Thus, I am lashing out at Lovey. I truly cannot stand the unjust and unfair way WHITE PEOPLE RUN THE EARTH.

WHO GAVE THEM ANY AUTHORITY TO RUN EARTH?

No Lovey. Why can't Mother Earth take back her land, food, water, everything that belongs to her from White People; all who are wicked and evil that fall under the WHITE BANNER OF DEATH?

And yes, I know that was a stupid question because; it's <u>humans who elected demons to kill them; take all life from them.</u>

Humans did elect demons to take their fundamental human rights from them.

Humans did elect demons to kill them literally.

Humans did elect demons to lie to them as wall as, deceive them.

Humans did elect demons to take them to hell with them.

Humans did elect demons to rape and rob them of their self worth and worth.

So yes, I am fed up.
Fed up of Mother Earth.
Fed up of Lovey and God.
Fed up of my life and the constant pain I am in.

Just fed up all around. I cannot go to the place I want to be in because if I do, <u>HELL WILL BECOME AND BE MY SPIRITUAL HOME ONCE MY SPIRIT SEPARATE FROM THE FLESH.</u>

So yes, *<u>I AM LASHING OUT AT HOW STUPID AND GULLIBLE WE AS BLACK PEOPLE ARE</u>*

BECAUSE; WE AS BLACK PEOPLE HELP THESE BC DEMONS TO DESTROY US AND LAND.

WE AS BLACK PEOPLE HELP THESE BC DEMONS TO DESTROY OUR LIFE ON LAND, OUR LIFE WITH GOD, OUR LIFE IN THE SPIRITUAL REALM, AND MORE.

WE AS BLACK PEOPLE ARE SUFFERING AND WE REFUSE TO COME TOGETHER TRUTHFULLY TO HELP EACH OTHER SO WE CAN LIVE RIGHT AND TRUE WITH OUR BLACK GOD.

No man, yes; *bleep Black People because we are all dumb asses.* WE BUILD OTHER NATIONS AND REFUSE TO BUILD US GOOD AND TRUE.

No, why the bleep should we have to suffer, and stay under COLONIAL LIES, RELIGIOUS LIES, WHITE LIES, BLACK LIES, EVERY BC NEGATIVITY THAT IS OUT THERE?

WHY THE BC DO WE HAVE TO STAY UNDER IT ALL?

BLEEP NOW MAN COME ON NOW.

I want to leave, and I cannot leave because; *GOD TOO IS TAKING AWAY MY GOD GIVEN RIGHT AND FUNDAMENTAL HUMAN RIGHTS HERE ON EARTH TO LIVE FREE, BE FREE, BE DEBT FREE, BE PAIN AND OR, HEALTH WOES FREE, AND MORE.*

You are God then be my God good and true.

Be the good and true God I need you to be all around.

Lead me good, true, clean, and right to the environment I need to be in so that *I CAN TRULY LIVE GOOD AND CLEAN ALL AROUND WITHOUT THE NEGATIVES OF LIFE COME ON NOW.*

No, I did not sign up FOR GOD SUFFERING.

I DID NOT SIGN UP FOR GOD PAIN.

I DID NOT SIGN UP FOR SPIRITUAL SUFFERING.

I DID NOT SIGN UP FOR DEATH.

I DID NOT SIGN UP FOR PHYSICAL PAIN.

I DID NOT SIGN UP FOR YOU GOD TO MUZZLE ME.

<u>I DID NOT SIGN UP TO BE A BITCH TO ANYONE COME ON NOW.</u>

I need permanent solutions to all my issues and that you as Lovey and God cannot do or give me; why?

Mi a yu puppunennay Lovey?

Mi a yu bitch that you can use and abuse at will?

I am more than categorically fed up of the constant pain I am in.

I am more than fed up of the worse than bitch nigger life I am living with you.

If you cannot be good and true to me then bleeping step then; leave. I've had it with you and the bullshit I have to face living here on Earth, and you are not truly listening to me or hearing me when it comes to me and my health issues; woes.

I need permanent solutions. Solutions you can give and refuse to give. So yes, this is my true Negative Day due to pain.

Why the hell should I live in pain?

Why the hell should I have to constantly eat shit; di dutty food wey dem gi wi fi food?

I want and need to plant my own food organically; truly natural and you Lovey is and are hindering me every step of the way because in my view, *YOU DON'T WANT ME TO BE HAPPY IN LIFE.*

YOU CAN'T STAND TO SEE ME BE HAPPY. YOU CAN'T STAND TO SEE ME BE FREE.

I am not your damned caged bird or animal. I am human with true needs and wants here on Earth. True needs and wants you do not want or need me to have, and I am truly BC fed up of your bullshit life.

No wonder people leave your ass because you cannot see beyond you and your needs.

Yes, I went there because I am angry and yes, those words are spiteful, but I truly do not care today if you are truly angry at me. I am fed up of my BC pain that I am constantly in and you are not helping me truthfully to get to where I need to be where I can live a decent life pain free, and more.

No one should have to eat nasty inorganic food that is filled with chemicals. I need true balance physically and spiritually Lovey come on now.

And yes, truly forgive me for being spiteful because I really and truly cannot deal with the pain I am in on most days. *Yes, you've helped me pain wise,* but I need a permanent solution to this constant pain, and all my health woes.

So yes Lovey, *in all the wicked and evil do globally they taint it all so that the good and true cannot live clean; no one can live good and true; clean here on Earth.* Thus, you Lovey cannot reside amongst your people here on Earth due to cleanliness.

Yes, it's a sad day for me because later I have to go to my dad's, and the back pain is just too great but somehow, I have to make it; get there.

It's difficult but I have to do what I need to do right now. My sons mainly, my eldest son painted the kitchen yesterday. It's my room now that need to be painted. He has some pain left over and I am going to paint over a section of my wall, and hopefully get another can of paint later on to finish up. Yes, my first preference is to leave this building by unfortunately, I cannot afford to move due to my mountainous debt load. Thus, owing Death Financially literally.

Debt Free is the way to go for me.

I better go make something to eat before I walk Queenie. And I am so going to take two Tylenols not that they truly help me.

I need to get natural anti-inflammatory medicine like ginger.

I have no energy plus at times my bones hurt.

Yes, this is my nightmare life period.

Michelle
July 12, 2021

It's July 16, 2021, and I thought I was done with this book, but I guess not. Yesterday I wanted to finish off my final edit to upload on Lulu.com but could not do this. I got no work done to how cool and breezy my room was.

I will not complain because my body was well comfortable throughout the day and evening. I have two other books pending and I do not know when I am going to complete these books. These books will be tame to what you are used to when it comes to my writings.

This I wrote yesterday morning.

When a company, the government, anyone manufacture weapons, diseases, viruses that maim and kill; are they not knowingly, and willingly committing murder?

Do the owners, governments, employees not legally get away with murder?

So now tell me, why do the Laws of Men protect these criminals from Death and Prison?

Why is it; the average citizen is charged for murder, and these Monsters; Demons get away with vile acts?

Why are they above the law?

Should they not be charged for Murder and Premeditated Murder?

Thus, the Law and Laws of Men protect the guilty and Society just go along with it.

That was what I wrote yesterday. However, I cannot worry about the guilty; Corporate Murderers, Government Murderers, or Employees that knowingly and willingly work for these Monsters; Murderers because; *many here on Earth, hath no moral values, ethical values, life values, and more.*

HUMANS LIVE FOR DEATH. THUS, DEATH'S PEOPLE RULE EARTH, MURDER AT WILL, AND GET AWAY WITH IT.

Death's Children and People truly do not think of Hell because; in all Death's Children and People do, they do all to bypass their Hell thus, *forgiveness, and them paying out Blood and or, Death Money to those they've erred.*

Humans are fooled by the White Race because in all the devil do and does:

THEY FAIL TO REALIZE, NO ONE CAN BYPASS DEATH; THEIR HELL IF THEIR NAME IS WRITTEN IN THE BOOK OF DEATH.

THEY FURTHER FAIL TO REALIZE THAT; DISOBEDIENCE IS AUTOMATIC DEATH ONCE

THE SPIRIT SHED THE FLESH. So, in all they do to bypass Hell; their death in Hell, they cannot.

THEY FAIL TO REALIZE THAT LIES TOLD ON GOD ONLY GOD CAN FORGIVE.

THEY FAIL TO REALIZE AND SEE, GENERATIONAL SINS DO CARRY FORWARD; THUS, MANY OF OLD; THEIR GENERATIONS OF OLD HAS AND HAVE LOCKED THEM OUT OF THE BOOK OF LIFE AND THE REALM OF LIFE WITH GOD LITERALLY.

Therefore, I will not worry about Death's Wicked and Evil Own because; I know the hell they must face literally.

I know the beating some receive and is going to receive in the grave.

I know the Demons of Hell thus, woe be unto them; the White Race literally.

Yesterday my sister called in the late evening which is not normal for my sister to do. We got to talking about the pain I am in, and she told me she was in the hospital for pain and that the pain medication they gave her did not work.

Listen, people's body are becoming immune to pain medications. I was also telling her about my pain because it came up in the conversation. She told me to take Tylenol Arthritis medication that helped her with her pain. I told her

I was the only one home and she said to call my last child and let him go pick some up for me. Suffice it to say I never did.

She was also telling me about Epsom Salt and something else that I tried. Should have never done that especially at night. The pain I was in. Trust me. *My body took on a full beating pain wise, sleep wise, and more.* Then to have these dreams for which you will see, read about just now.

Like I said; it's July 16, 2021, and I thought I was done with this book, but I guess not.

I cannot worry about White People because; *THEY ARE CONDEMNED.*

Now this dream.

I was somewhere. I cannot tell you where, but I was with this younger looking White Guy. He was good looking nor did he have a bad shape. I can't remember if he had a priest uniform on and or, a suit. Anyway, where we were, it was as if John Forsythe was there, but John Forsythe was not there. You could not see him; John Forsythe. I do not know what the White Guy said if he lied on me but upon finding out what he did, *"I CONDEMNED HIM TO HELL."* He was shocked that I would condemn him to hell but said not a word to me.

After I condemned him to hell, did the Demons of Hell take shape and fold here on Earth in the form of *YOUNG FEMALE WHITE VAMPIRES?*

Yes

They went on a feeding frenzy for which I had to stop them. There were people in this car and this one particular Young White Female Vampire attacked the people in the car. But the weird part of it was, *she had turned the occupants of the car into people of old then back to the present.* And yes, I did stop her from harming and or, feeding on the occupants of the car.

I truly do not know how to analyze this dream.

I do not know if I was in the grave, a cemetery, hell, what. All I know is, I was condemning this White Guy to Hell therefore, I know for a fact *WHITE PEOPLE ARE CONDEMNED TO HELL.*

YES, I CONDEMNED THEM; THIS WHITE MAN THUS, HELL CAME UPON EARTH.

Listen, I do not know if this condemnation will stick or if all in the White Race is fully and truly condemned. I can't remember if the dream scared me. But for me. *OLD DEATH IS NEW DEATH, and with HER SHOWING ME THE PAST; PEOPLE OF OLD THEN BACK TO REALITY IF THIS*

<u>IS HELL'S WAY; THE DEMONS OF HELL WAY OF TELLING ME THAT WHITE PEOPLE ARE CONDEMNED FROM THE PAST TO THE PRESENT INCLUDING THE FUTURE.</u>

Further, I do not know if this man was Satan, I was condemning to Hell thus, Hell came down to Earth and or, upon Earth.

Now my other dream had to do with water. I was somewhere. I cannot tell you where because I truly do not know. All I know is. I was in Water Yogurt Pink Water. I Googled Yogurt Pink and that pink you see is the exact pink of the water I was in.

There were Black Children in the water.

Now I wanted to float in the water and the water carried me away from the others; children. I could not swim, and it dawned on me that I could not swim so this young Black Guy came to my rescue by leading me safely to shore. In the water there was this huge hippo. I think I was scared; did not want to move lest the hippo charge us. Then I was with this young Black Female, and I believe we were talking.

Oh God, <u>*I do not know if this Yogurt Pink Water represent hell,*</u> and I am being rescued from Hell literally.

I do not know if this river and or water is in Africa, but I would assume so, and I truly do not want or need to assume.

I KNOW FOR A FACT WITHOUT DOUBT GOD IS GOING TO WALK AWAY FROM AN AFRICAN LAND BECAUSE AFRICANS ARE NOT WALKING IN THE WAY OF GOD AND LIFE.

AFRICANS HAVE AND HAS ABANDONED THE TRUE AND RIGHT WAY OF LIFE. THEREFORE, AFRICA; AFRICANS KEEP THE LIES OF DEATH.

Yes, there is more Africans are guilty of, but I've talked about Africans *TELLING THE TRUTH OF SLAVERY IN OTHER BOOKS.*

AFRICANS NEED TO TELL THE TRUTH. Therefore, I truly do not know if the Yogurt Pink Water IN SPIRITUAL HELL COMING DOWN TO EARTH TO DEVOUR AN AFRICAN LAND.

I cannot speculate because I truly do not know. *I know Africa and Africans are not safe because; A LOT OF ILLS IS HAPPENING IN THAT LAND.*

TOO MANY DISTORTED; VILE, DISGUSTING, AND WICKED LEADERS RESIDE IN AFRICA

THAT HAVE AND HAS CARRIED OUT VILE ACTS OF CRIME, THEFT, INJUSTICE, AND MORE WHEN IT COMES TO THEIR PEOPLE AND FOR THIS; MANY IN AFRICA AND THE LAND OF AFRICA MUST PAY. AFRICANS DID BREAK THE LAWS OF LIFE.

AFRICANS DID ABANDON LIFE.

AFRICANS DID ABANDON THEIR BLACK GOD.

AFRICANS DID FORFEIT THEIR BLACK KNOWLEDGE.

AFRICANS DID FORFEIT THE TRUTH OF LIFE FOR EVIL.

THEREFORE, GOD IS TRULY NOT PLEASED WITH AFRICA NOR IS MOTHER AFRICA PLEASED WITH HER PEOPLE. And yes, MOTHER AFRICA DID ASK ME FOR PRAYER YEARS AGO AND PRAYER WAS GIVEN UNTO HER BY ME.

You will not comprehend this, because you truly do not know the different worlds; realms spiritually and what the Spirit; well, my Spirit can and cannot do.

Those who are of Life; walking truthfully with God has and have access to all Life. And, it matters not if that Life is Death.

Those who are of Life can command Death. Therefore, I tell you. Blacks must unite good and true.

If Blacks do not unite good and true, Blacks would have failed Life.

"TRUE UNITY IS A MUST FOR BLACK PEOPLE IF WE WANT TO BE SAVED FROM ALL OF THIS." Yes, all that is happening on Earth and all that is to come shortly before 2032.

After that dream, my other dream had to do with this rickety and ratchet looking Old White Man that was yuk to me. Think homeless and yuk; nasty. He was laying beside me, and he had his foot around me. Just all out gross.

That dream I will leave alone because it is just all out gross and yuk.

After that I dream, I was in another place. High up. There was this wall, and the cutest little things; think babies but you could not see the faces. Google babies wrapped together but more so Russian Dolls wrapped together in Google Images. Russian Dolls wrapped together is the image that would best describe what these two little things looked like without a face.

There was this not brick but, mortared stone wall before me and or, stone wall, and the little things; babies without a face fell over the wall and down the hill; grassy hill. They did not die nor were they hurt. They just made their way back up the hill using another path. Nor were they separated when they fell over the wall. I know one baby was specifically dressed in red, and I believe the other was dressed in blue.

I will not analyze that dream because I truly do not know what it means therefore, I am leaving it alone.

Sleep wise, pain wise, sweat wise, all around wise, my night was hell. And I am so going to leave everything alone. Please, live clean, take care of yourself, and do all that is good and true; positive for you.

It's almost 9:30am and I have not walked my dog. Asked my last child to walk Queenie for me yesterday.

When I inquired if he walked Queenie, he did not walk her.

He said Queenie did not like him.

I said, she didn't want to go with you?

He said yes.

This is typical of Queenie. When I am home, I am the one to walk her. She will refuse to go for a walk with my last child and or, give problems. Thus, I know my dog.

Managed to walk her and God I almost fainted outside. It was by the Grace of God I made it back home to the amount of pain I was in.

Inside, at the door; I had to scream out for help as the tears came. The pain was that bad to the point of almost falling.

My sons helped me to my bed, but I could not lay down. I had to sit up literally. Now, I am sitting up writing and my son; last one is going to get my prescription and or, referral for the Chiropractor tor me.

Yesterday, my back was so not having it. The pain got to the point where I could not move my right leg, and I could not walk my dog the second time around.

Michelle

BOOKS WRITTEN BY MICHELLE JEAN 2021

MY TALK JANUARY 2021

MY TALK JANUARY 2021 – BOOK TWO

MINI BOOK

JUST TALKING – THINKING

A LITTLE TALK WITH MOTHER EARTH

I NEED ANSWERS GOD

POETRY MY WAY

THE MIND AND SPIRITUALITY

I NEED ANSWERS GOD – PART TWO

MY NIGHTS

I NEED ANSWERS GOD – PART THREE

GOD IS GOOD

WHAT ABOUT US

WOW WHAT

AFRICAN – BLACK PEOPLE CUSS OUT

THE FIFTH WAVE – BLACK PEOPLE WARNING

FINAL CALL

JUST MY TALK 2021

THE TRAP

CHANGES

COMING SOON
GIVE ME A REASON – SPIRITUAL CLEANSING

LIFE AFTER DEATH